G000320269

Reflections of the Soul

A POETRY ANTHOLOGY

Spiritual Writers Network

Presents

Reflections of the Soul

A Poetry Anthology

ISBN-10: 0615863469
ISBN-13: 978-0-615-86346-7

Transcendent Publishing

Reflections of the Soul: A Poetry Anthology

This collection of poetry is dedicated to all the talented souls who contribute to Spiritual Writers Network.

TABLE OF CONTENTS

Introduction

Introduction

"To elevate the soul, poetry is necessary."
~ Edgar Allan Poe

When I launched Spiritual Writers Network in February 2013, I never imagined the growth the website would encounter in such a short amount of time. In just a few months, the site has grown to over a thousand writers and poets who collectively publish and share their short stories and poems on the network each and every day.

When I originally created the site, I added several categories for the authors to place their short stories into. I very quickly realized there were many talented poets sharing their poetry on the site as well. This led me to add a category solely for poetry, and now that category is the fastest growing on the network.

It is my mission to broaden the stage for the writers of Spiritual Writers Network, and that is why I run quarterly contests for publication. When the time came to announce the second quarter writing contest for publication, I knew beyond a shadow of a doubt that the writers and poets of the network would benefit greatly from a poetry competition. For this contest, we received several wonderful submissions from many great poets, and this anthology is a collection of those poems.

I admire these poets for writing so openly about their emotions, life experiences, joys and hardships. It was such a pleasure to compile this anthology for them, and when choosing a theme for the book only one phrase came to mind -- *Reflections of the Soul.* These writers have put their hearts and souls into these poems for you to enjoy. I hope you will find as much delight and admiration for this collection of works as I have.

Blessings,
Shanda Bisanz
Founder, Spiritual Writers Network
www.spiritualwritersnetwork.com

I Am the Gentle Rain that Falls

By Bernadette Price

I'm sorry I had to leave you

I'm sorry I had to go

My time here has passed now

But there are some things I want you to know

As you stand by my grave and weep

While I am being buried deep

Remember, it is just my body that has died

For I am always by your side

I am the rainbow that appears after the rain

I am the lambs that gambol on the plain

I am the sweet smile on your child's face

I am the flowers that dance with such grace

As the winds they whisper through the trees

I am the waves that crash the mighty seas

I am the gentle rain that falls in Summer

I am the tender kiss of a dear lover

And when you look upwards to the night sky

You will notice me by the naked eye

For I am that Star that shines so bright

Yes, I am that Star: your guiding light

I want you to know that I am all these things

My comfort to you, I will bring

Until the day we are united again

Just think of me as that Gentle Rain

Bernadette is a Spiritualist medium/ clairvoyant and writer, whose background is in Angelic work and Reiki healing. Bernadette is finally living her dream in a beautiful village in Cheshire, England, and she loves nothing better than going for a run in the open air whilst mentally writing her next article or poem, and is currently working on her first book which she hopes to get published one day before she falls off her perch.

When she is not doing that she loves to spend time in the company of her great friends, lovely fella, Dave and feeding her adolescent son, Adrian, and being his taxi driver.

http://workwiththeangels.weebly.com
https://www.facebook.com/pages/Work-with-the-Angels

What a Wondrous Day
By Pol Macmathuna

What a wondrous day

The day

The little boy came out to play

He wandered through the bluebell clumps

To sit beneath whispering trees

And even heard the swallows

Call his name apon the breeze

For many years, A lifetime

He had sat in a prison cell

Its walls were made of voices

That told him he was bold

Its bars were made of teardrops

Gathered from wounds of old

But led by the master

And helped to stand

By Growers hands

The little boy in the man

Felt safe

To come out and play

And when the joy of a child within us

Is set free from its prison cell

Life becomes a jewel

Heaven sent for you and me.

Poetry as a form of self expression can be inspirational and act as music for the soul.

Having been in recovery for many years and with the nurturing encouragement of Peer support group Grow Ireland the seed of writing was planted in my heart. This poem is a fruit of that seed.

Dublin taxi driver by night. Writer and poet by day. Educated to degree level in the Natural sciences at Trinity College Dublin. Influences are the natural world, science, and a spirituality which comes from deep personal experience of Life. Finds expression of a rich inner life in creative writing and poetry.

Your Mini Me

By Rylee Rioux Blanchard

I'll never have to say goodbye

I know you'll never leave

They say you're in a special place

So I don't need to grieve

I won't forget your big bear hugs

That took my tears away

Or how you always listened close

To every word I'd say

It was you who would defend me

You're still my bestest friend

You always were so proud of me

And told me 'til the end

I'm thankful for the gift of YOU

And every single day

I'm so proud you are my dad

And wish that you could stay

I'll always be your Honey Bunny

And you're my beating heart

I won't say goodbye to you

'Cause we will never part

We'll be together every day

In each other's thoughts

In all the words I ever write

In all our favorite spots

I would give up all my toys

To see you one more time

Just to hug you once again

Or feel your hand on mine

I won't forget the many times

You looked into my eyes

The last I ever saw you

When you kissed away my cries

Now I see you everyday

Each time that I see ME

Mommy says my eyes are yours

So I know that they must be

And even though they turn to slits

With every grin I crack

That's when I love my face the most

'Cause YOU are looking back

I just want to hold you tight

And never let you go

My world stopped completely

When mommy let me know

Tears fell down my cheeks like rain

I couldn't talk at all

I wanted to jump in your arms

Where I would never fall

I thought I was inside a dream

And sometimes I still do

But I'm so glad when people look at me

And they see YOU!

Thank you so much Daddy

For all the times we had

The greatest gift I ever got

Was you to be my DAD

The hardest thing I'd ever have to do

Is say "Goodbye"

Instead let's keep our pinky promise

To always just say "Hi"

I know someday we'll hug again

In Heaven where you'll be

'Til then I'll see you in my mirror

'Cause I'm your MINI ME

Dedicated to my Dad James R Blanchard (12/18/72 - 04/24/13)

Rylee Rioux Blanchard, born April 8th, 2003, is entering the 5th grade at Huffaker Elementary School in Reno Nevada. She loves to write poetry, song lyrics, and short stories. Rylee has been writing and illustrating her own books since she was only 3 years old. She and her dad have written many children's books together over the years, just for fun. She was heart-broken when he passed away in April this year. The two of them bonded through her passion for Creative Writing. He was so very proud of his "Honey Bunny."

I Shed a Tear for Boston

By Sonnia J. Kemmer

I shed a tear of sadness
For the city of Boston
I wasn't there and felt useless
But life must go on

I shed a tear while praying
For the city of Boston
With closed eyes hoping
That lives will move on

I shed a tear of control
For the city of Boston
To erase people's vitriol
No more rage to happen

I shed a tear of peace
For the city of Boston
Their love to increase
And care to function

I shed a tear for Boston
Will you do the same?
To clearly have a vision
Without blame, without shame

Every state
Without hate
Shed a tear
Right here
Right now

Sonnia J. Kemmer is the author of "Sonnia's Sonnets" self-published through www.lulu.com. She is currently a Freelance Writer for Yahoo Contributor Network. She's also one of Cindi Myers' students through Long Ridge Writers Group where she's taking up "Breaking Into Print." She writes science-fiction fantasy during her spare time and exchanges snail mail with numerous pen pals around the world.

Resurrection

By Debbie Aycock Williams

The leaves are gone as bare branches

solicit the Heavens

The warm days are spent as

lingering blades of grass glisten

From the morning frost

seeking absolution from their iniquities

Ensuing eradication

wounds the external covering

And when they have relented at last

the hope of resurrection

Rests in the seed

Reflections of the Soul: A Poetry Anthology

That was scattered

Long ago...

Constant Current

By Kathleen M. Regan

In-between the banter and the angst,

there's a place I have been led to

over waves of time.

Time ... consisting of moments

dangerously thunderous in one breath,

blessedly healing in the next,

like a wave capsizing me

one moment,

washing me clean

the next.

Oh, this place ... this place I have been

led to over waves of time

holds an ebb and flow

always in sight

of its shoreline,

its safe harbor a beacon of Peace

uplifted by Shaman's smoke, Holy;

grounded in Earth rituals, Blessed;

enlivened by conscious breath, Witnessed;

empowered by soul-seated prayer,

Beseeching,

Praising,

Thanking.

You see, within this place

I have been led to

over waves of time

there runs a river,

its rippling inhale and exhale

a constant current,

womb-deep and

sacred ...

steady, yet flowing ...

always flowing

in-between

the banter and

the angst.

The Eye of the Storm

By Wendy Sammut

Around me whirls chaos.

Within me scattered thinking.

If I am pulled in one more direction I will scream.

My breath catches in my throat

My heart is pounding

Anxiety fills me with panic and dread

I feel as if I will implode.

"Focus Wendy", "Breathe Wendy".

Deep within the recesses of my mind I hear the voices

Distant at first, barely audible

My brain swirls as they become louder, more insistent

The chaos threatens to overwhelm.

I hold my breath; afraid to let it go, afraid to breathe

Afraid another breath will not arrive

But it does.

Hesitant at first, uncertain, it catches in my throat

Ever so slowly it leaves and with it the tiniest bit of fear

I feel my neck and shoulders relax slightly.

My mind, like a predator, sees the movement and tenses

Becomes still, observant, on guard

Waiting to attack at any moment

The breath continues to cautiously arrive and hesitantly leave

The mind gradually backs down

The threat lessons

Slowly, gingerly the anxiety eases

I become the eye of the storm.

Wendy Sammut is a thinker, a dreamer, a wannabe writer. Having spent over 20 years journaling, studying eastern philosophy, teaching and exploring yogic practices, she has come to a place of needing to voice her thoughts. Through articles, poetry and short stories she presents her experiences and ponderings to the reader. Teaching traditional hatha yoga and meditation since 1996 that includes specialized work for the Mississauga M.S. Society, CMHA-Halton Region she has developed a great understanding of the relationship between the body and the mind.

Detach

By April Coldsmith

We sit round the table

cradling our issues

like a dog bites

to protect his wounded paw.

Guru says,

too much emotion.

Detach.

He doesn't even know what that means.

I know what it is not.

I sit by the bed of a dying little one

and smell roses

lotion her mother rubbed in

tiny hands the hour before -

Perfume to cover darkness.

Eight year old fingers grasp mine

and we make a tender blossom on the eve of spring.

Her mother paces

Aimless, hoping

activity will make all the difference.

Their love sweetens me

How can I detach.

Rev. April Coldsmith is a minister in the Presbyterian Church(U.S.A.). As a medical chaplain, she has worked with children and adults at end-of-life for fifteen years. She previously published articles in the Other Side, Insights and the Presbyterian Sun. She blogs at Me, Breaking In, www.facebook.com/aprilDcoldsmith and www.aprilcoldsmith.blogspot.com.

Believe

By Holly Grantham

There is magic stirring in the deep places

while sweaty heads sleep

and grown brows furrow

In a twinkling

up is turned down

in is flipped out

And love spills warm and gentle

into the cracks

hewn from worry

For this magic

that is unseen

It has a force

all its own

And no manner of flailing

or gnashing of teeth

No turning away

or arms crossed defiant

Can turn it away

or disfigure its

joy tinged face

with angst and vexing

No, it has come

this magic

And all we must ever do

is hear the whisper

from down deep

that says

I believe.

Holly is a wife, very relaxed homeschooling mom of two boys, snapper of photos, coming of age writer and a soul drowning in grace. After years in Atlanta where she attended college, married the love of her life and lived in an intentional community, she found her way back to her home state of Missouri. She now lives in an antebellum stone house, raises chickens (sometimes) and pretends that she lives in the country.

Divine Light

By Agnes Tai

God, You are my Light!

You illuminate me, you illuminate us.

I was born to the world, you smile to me.

I am happy, you strongly shine up for me.

I am worried and sadness, you unconditionally send love to me.

I walk on the darkness, you unlimitedly protect and guide me.

I can't live without you, I can't live without you!

Your light brings to the world with Souls.

Your light gives to everything with Love.

Your light is full of powerful Wisdom.

Your light makes every individual Contented.

Your light indicates to us in right ways.

We follow your direction.

We are living in your arms very safely.

We have given you without any hesitation.

We are infinitely grateful and blissful with you.

We love You! We love You!

Let us serve you now.

Let us seed your light to grow everywhere.

Let us spread your light to soak with Mother Earth together.

Let us continue to extend your light to future generations.

Let us say to thank you wholeheartedly!

Thank you, God.

Sun on the Rapids

By Gary Bennet

A honey light dances where

the waters are clear. The fringes

are framed in foam. A face

floats along the flow in a constant,

never wavering pose. No matter the

froth, regardless of what swims under.

That is the natural state of things, with

light laying a golden glaze on what lies

beneath. My mother taught me that in

her brightest smiles. Her eyes would hold

me steady as the foam framed her. You only

saw the light dance when the darkness fell.

Gary Wayne Bennett is a native of Memphis, Tennessee now living in Jonesboro, Arkansas. He is a graduate of Southwest Tennessee Community College. Ten years ago, he began a lifetime dedication to daily writing. It is his belief we are never alone in this life. He dedicates his poem to Angels of three faces: One named Marla June Utley, another named Jamie Sharissa Peeler, and the third he calls mom...

A Wanderer's Soul

By Matthew Pensyl

I wander because I am a searcher
I search because I know there is beauty to be found
I live because I love
I love because that is all that matters
I weep because I must move on
I smile because I carry memories
I remember because it

is my story
I tell the story because it is also Our story
I get lost because I wander

I wander because I am a searcher.

*On 31January2010, Petty Officer 1*st *Class Matt Pensyl retired from over 21 years of service to the United States Navy. He served as an Air Traffic Controller primarily, but also attended SEAL training, EOD training (Bomb Disposal/Dive school), served 3 years as a Military Policeman in Naples, Italy, and wrapped up his final 6 years as a Navy Career/Guidance Counselor.*

Matt immediately embarked on a journey to finding Self via higher education at the University of Minnesota and at Boise State University. Through this journey, it was apparent that a switch to massage therapy school and energy healing modalities were most congruent with his path to true happiness and Self. Writing his progress publicly via social media proved to be the voice that Matt needed, and he is excited to watch the words flow from Source for creation of his abundance and sharing of his part of the Life story!

The Anima Initiation

By Lydia Fraser

She speaks through the lovers of silence

Seeking her presence, disperses defiance

Professing one's purity, the need to feel whole

Bathe in the depths of her eternal soul...

The embryonic waters promote self-healing

A symbiotic state of veritable feeling

Do not fear drowning, for her waters are still

Immerse thy self, be receptive to her will

Her universal solvent, strips us to the bone

Vulnerability sanctions reliance, in trusting the unknown

Through her initiation, she asks that you receive

The origins of self.... In which to believe.

I wrote this poem when my mother was diagnosed with cancer.
Towards the end of her life she explained to me that she rejected her
religion because it lacked the 'feminine aspect'. This poem is about my
journey in relation to embracing the 'inner goddess'. I dedicate this

poem to my mum.

Peacocks at a Fountain

by Tazeem Moledina

His arm is exquisite

honey-gold, and inked

with geometric petals.

They spiral and creep

deliciously upward,

then slink away beneath

a blood-red sleeve.

Hot.

They study each other

at the water cooler:

His boy-brown eyes,

matching stubble;

a peacock feather

in her hair.

"Like Lord Krishna,"

he smiles.

She shakes her head,

fills her water bottle;

gazes.

"But you must know that,

you're Indian…"

She hears him and

wants to stroke,

in circles, the

etched stamens

on his left wrist

with her fingertips.

"I'm Indian, but I only know

about the buttermilk.

Tell me".

Eyes naked, he says:

"I went to Rishikesh

really messed up…

studied the Gita

to get off drugs."

She watches his lips

and thinks of kisses,

then glimpses teeth,

yellow-grey and worn.

Their souls lock

Into a *mala*, and

when he slightly bows,

she wordlessly, easily

breathes him in.

TAZEEM MOLEDINA was born in Perivale, West London in 1971 and spent her formative years in NW London suburbia. As a child she wrote and published two poems for her mosque magazine. Aged 18 she spread her adolescent wings by moving up North - to Merseyside for 9 years, where she studied Politics and Media at Liverpool University, followed by a Masters degree in Children and Families Social Work. Tazeem then worked full-time in children's social care in London until 2 years ago - since when she has slowly and tenderly been re-discovering her first and truest loves: the written word, and herself.

Symmetria   (for David Ligare)

By Robert Smith

These, almost pictures into the mind of God:

Hubble to Earth of dancing galaxies, a symmetria

Of possibilities: but how does one begin to imagine

The force that protects the balance of everything?

A single black crow descends to the ground,

A single orange butterfly wings past the window,

And the green pines wave in the silent spring wind:

Perhaps the entire ocean can fit into this single red bowl...

Perhaps, too, adoration is best for Mystery:

How else to live upon this precious blue Planet?

Raindrops begin to tap against the window,

As if calling through mind to see the hidden jewels...

Each moment is another picture, another conclusion,

Birthing a completely new beginning, and another movement

Reflections of the Soul: A Poetry Anthology

Into the magic of the Universe, into the music of Only One:

The Love that protects the balance of everything...

Hands of Destiny

by Elizabeth Vaccaro

I look into the face of a rhythmic destiny,
And before me a vision of the heavenly.
Divine timing and justice have been off-course...
Do I turn back to catch up, or do I feel remorse?
Can winding back destiny's hands reverse time?
Or, will it just instil a longer waiting line?
Both then and now would make my soul complete...
Do I move backwards or forwards for these hands to meet?

Elizabeth Vaccaro is a philosophy author, and astrology columnist for Goddess Guru Magazine of BlackRose Publishing. Her subjects of interest include the laws of nature, macrocosmic/microcosmic philosophy, science, enchantment, natural medicines, dance, and music. To email Elizabeth Vaccaro, write to sheri.elizabeth@live.com.au. Her website and blogs can be found at www.elizabethvaccaro.com, www.facebook.com/enchanted.healing, and https://twitter.com/GoddessStars.

Things I Love or Didn't Know I Loved

By Janet R. Sady

I always knew I loved the creek for the way it meanders,
like an unfurling ribbon, filling inlets and crannies.

I never knew I loved the rocks, which protrude from the creek bed
churning water as it pummels jagged edges.
Perhaps, I really only love the white foam
because it reminds me of my hazelnut cappuccino.

I knew I loved the blue heron who visits my creek every summer.
He stands on one skinny-stick leg, while dipping for trout and
crayfish.

I never knew I loved the Turtle-head flowers, discovered quite by
accident
along the creek bank—all creamy pink with flattened heads.

I knew I loved the purple violets—"Johnny Jump Ups,"
which flourish along the creek path. And I love their snow-white
and lemon cousins, which have the audacity to be called violets,
when there's not a trace of purple in them.

I never knew I loved the briars.
Tentacles of thorns reach out to snag my skin and jacket.
I loved the briars when they grew delicate white blossoms,
and then changed clothes to become ebony blackberries.

I knew I loved the swimming holes and the low places,
where I can wade with jean legs rolled up,
wearing sneakers—full of holes. Shoes, Mom saved for just such
purpose.

I knew I loved the creek in which I drop my canoe.
For the way in which it carried me downstream on summer afternoons—
drifting far from conflict.

I never knew I loved the creek best for its faithfulness, until I moved far way.
It was there when I returned—a constant, always doing what it was meant to do—
flowing on, in an ever changing world.

Janet R. Sady is an award-winning author, poet, story teller, and motivational speaker. She is published in devotional books and other anthologies, newspapers, and magazines, including, but not limited to: Falling in Love with You, I Choose You, Secret Place, Penned from the Heart, Country Woman, Loyalhanna Review, True Story, Alamance Magazine etc. Janet is the author of the Great American Dream, God's Lessons from nature, God's Parables, The Bird Woman, Mr. Bernie's Most Favorite Place, and Winston Wants a Home for Christmas. Read her inspirational blogs at: jansady422.wordpress.com

A Million White Feathers
By Sue Daniels

On my own I sit, I still see your face in the distance

You've gone while memories hang bare and the old clock chimes

Remembering your smell, your skin from ages old,

Oh Mum, I've laughed and cried in your arms so many times

'Just wait to see a feather' I heard someone say

You'll know it was sent just for you

Don't dismiss it, don't deny it

I'm telling you, she'll be trying to get through

Well, a million white feathers will never bring you back to me

Your unconditional love has left my side

A million white feathers will never bring you back to me

The pain went deep, crushed my world, rivers I've cried

The grief cycle they call it, yeah round and round it goes

Head spinning dropping me to my knees

Time takes pain away; I know that's what people say

They have no idea what I've lost, but I know they will one day

Well, a million white feathers will never bring you back to me

Your unconditional love has left my side

A million white feathers will never bring you back to me

I've wished so many times you'd never died

When you see a feather she said it will be from up above

Keep it with you always and hang on to her love

Symbolic realms of angels are forever in our hearts

They keep the peace around us dove like flying darts

Well, a million white feathers will never bring you back to me

Your unconditional love has left my side

A million white feathers will never bring you back to me

Grief comes and goes like the changing of the tide

Sue Daniels is a keen writer, having had fiction and non-fiction published, she regularly writes for organizational projects on posttraumatic disorder, associated symptoms and related counseling topics as well as fictional short stories and poetry. Whatever she writes comes from her heart and her poignant love of the written word.

Blank Page

by Coleen Skinner

I stare at this blank page

What words will escape and fill it

Emotions stir deep below the surface

Do they need to be heard

I know my heart is heavy tonight

Filled with questions of what my tomorrow might bring

My heart and mind are quarrelling

Arguing about what is best for me

I stand here in this moment

Pulled in all directions

Both unsettling and all too familiar .

Battling between what is expected

And that of an old dream

I push myself in silence

While I cry on bended knee

Reminding myself of how I use to see

Desperately I try to silence the chatter

Searching for the courage that once lived in side of me

Has my faith become silent

As I hide here in my shadow

I stare at this blank page

Take from me my sorrow

Guide me back towards the light

Let my words open windows

So I may take flight

Guide me to where my courage lays

And help me to awaken my faith that sleeps

Ashes to Ashes

Dust to Dust

May I find the strength inside me

So I can lay this cowardly part of me to rest

May this blank page give me courage to write the beginning I see

May it give me wings to fly

To the places I have never been

May this blank page fill my spirit with hope

Giving me back the Faith

I had forgotten I hold

I will trust in the darkness

To bring me into the light

And this blank page

To resurrect the next chapter in my life

Annunciation

By Cynthia Schaub

If an angel really came
          to Mary,
if I believed that,

Was she the first he
          visited
or did he go door to door,
          checking
for virgins?
(Not so rare in those times.)

And if he came to me,
          would my response
be yes,
or a negotiation of
          perqs
for the favor of bearing
          a king?

Innocence and
          faith
bred out of us
in this modern life.

Those of you who believe,
is it faith, or will, or
grace?

Cynthia Strauff Schaub is a retired executive who has now allowed her left brain full authority. She has received numerous writing awards, and is the author of two books. She is currently working on a poetry chapbook, as well a historic novel set in Baltimore.

Memories

By Debbie Williams

A whiff of a long lost scent which clung to your tweed jacket
The one that you wrapped around my shoulders as we walked the
calles of Cali
The warmth of your arms permeating through the fabric unto my
skin
Left a scar that transcended into my heart

A scent that surrounds me with hope
Of which life comes full circle
And someday the aroma in the air will be
Of that tweed jacket and the arms tucked inside

Older now, the scent must be softer, more subtle
Tender yet worn from the years of wear and tear
But no less the scent in my memory
Of a closeness buried deep into the threads of that familiar garment

Forty years have passed and your voice transcends time
As you speak, I close my eyes your voice permeates my conscience
Your penetrating accent pulls me back in time
Slowly moving, pressed together in rhythm of the Kontiki's Latin
song

Did you say Rendezvous? Yes! Where? When?
Cartegena, Cool nights, ancient history, your blue tweed jacket
Arms wrapped around my shoulders as we stroll the narrow calles
Your wafted scent bringing me closer to what I thought was lost
forever

Veil

By Christian Luca

All we see and experience in life

is enshrouded by a misty veil,

Oh, but even the great strife

felt by some taken off to jail,

leaving behind loved ones and a wife—

is such an experience a veiled tale?

Oh, but when it comes to examining one's life,

it is a great mystery and its understanding tends to fail.

With such great and bold convictions,

we proceed to carry on and uphold them to flail

at the meritorious ideas as interdictions,

in the process rendering them stale,

so that we may continue in our addictions

fabricated in our minds to make everything discordant pale

in comparison with our own maledictions

that constitute the very life we all experience as a veil.

Into the Quiet

By Nancy Schenkel

Oh God~

    I want to write from my quiet place.

    No solemness or sadness there.

    Fill my face with your light.

    Fill my mouth with your words.

    Write your name across my breasts.

    Take my demons and show them compassion

        That they may harm no more.

    Keep me yours.

Even this, I turn to a dream. My prayer. My love. You made me feel so strong, so loved, so clean. And now I dream a dream. My prayer. My sweet prayer. I've tarnished you.

Oh God~

    Fill my mind with your love...

    Fill my mind with your love...

    Fill my mind...with you.

My Love~

    Taste the salt of your tears.

Know they are there...

Because you have sinned.

Know they are there...

Because you have repented.

Know they are there...

Because you have been forgiven.

Nancy is a Licensed Clinical Social Worker (LCSW) and a certified Spiritual Director. Her work as a social worker providing end of life care at a hospice has been a vehicle for learning a deeper sense of Spirit in her own journey of life. She enjoys sharing the Spirit through writing, painting, and needlework. Nancy is married to her soul-mate and considers herself blessed that God chose her and her husband to be the protectors and mentors of their two, now adult, children.

The Key to My Happiness

By Bernadette Price

It broke my heart the day love died

It broke my heart: I cried and cried

I know a lot of water has flowed under the bridge, but

I still recall there were a lot of things that drew a wedge

Between us

I really do wish you well

And as I watch our son grow

It makes my heart swell

With pride

In the years since the separation

And during times of deep contemplation

I have come to realise one important thing

And in a strange way, it makes my heart sing

You see, no other man will have the whole of my heart

No, no other man will be able to rip it apart, like you

It has taken some time to find the glue

To stick it together again

No, no other man will make me feel that much pain

I am finally free to just be me

I have finally found the key

To my happiness

Don't worry, I'm not saying you are the Devil

I wouldn't dream of calling you evil

But money does not keep you warm at night

There is no substitute for someone special who holds you tight

Old friend, I don't need a Lottery win to make me happy

Although it would be very welcome!

No, I don't need a Lottery win to be happy

Because I know it doesn't really make a happy home

I love to lock MY door at night

Knowing that this is MY home

It has helped empower me

To be the woman I have finally become

Finally free, to be ME

That is my key to being happy

Breathe Me to Life

~ A Sestina Variation

By Carolyn E. Ford

Thee see my scars,

Please don't turn away in disgust.

Thee see my wounds,

Please bind them so they can heal.

Thee see my tears,

Please gently touch them in compassion.

Thee see me as I am with compassion,

Please love me in spite of the scars.

Thee see my heart in tattered tears,

Please breathe Thy love without disgust

Thee see my fire-scorched soul in ashes and in Thy mercy,
Thee heal

Please breathe life in the dying embers of my wounds.

Bind with grace and place peace in my wounds.

Wrap me in your undying compassion.

In Thy arms, my soul softly is healed.

With one touch from Thee are healed every scar.

One look from Thy gaze takes away all disgust,

Wipes away every tear.

My heart alive beats once more amongst its tattered tears.

No longer ashes in my soul's wounds.

In the mirror I no longer see disgust.

I see in my eyes radiant with Thy compassion.

I rejoice that no residual is left from my scars.

I give Thee the utmost praise for I am healed.

Like the woman with the issue of blood that long ago Thee healed,

Distant from memory are my tears.

Marked in beauty are my scars.

My face, my soul, my heart are etched from healed wounds.

I lightly outlined these scars, these wounds with compassion.

No longer do I view these rites of passage with disgust.

Others may wonder why Thee see me without disgust.

Only we know with certainty that I am healed.

Only Thee, my Creator, have for me the wondrous compassion.

Thy love is only one soft fall away from a tear.

Courage speaks my wounds.

Resilience shouts my scars.

Yea, though I walk with a limp from my scars.

I bear proudly Thy grace in my wounds,

My face now wet in gratitude to Thee with my tears.

Breathe me to life.

The Flowering

By Pol Macmathuna

Once , Frightened and Alone

I watched

As the daffodils reached out

Through the cold earth of winter

I waited

In hope and longing

For the first buds to appear

Each day

It was my prayer

To look and see

The leaves grow slowly to the light

Like my growing self

A frozen winter bud

Longing to open

And be nourished by the light

Mental suffering has played a major part in my self realisation and in breaking some of the bonds of ego. This poem is a reflection on a time of intence emotional suffering when endurance was helped by focusing on the plants in the garden. In my mind I held onto a lifeline that if I could only endure untill the plants flowered in the spring my pain might have resolved.

Mother Divine

By Nithya Kavyaroopini

Oh Mother Divine!

Every time I think of you, how could it be this way

Your appearance in the mirror of the heart

As, how a moon would slowly peer through dark clouds into

The lake of intranquility, having its final say!

It is not meant to reflect the beauty, this heart of clay

But your moon gold presence imparts it a ray

Of pearly luminosity and creates

Its own reflection and raises me as if in a play!

Like the moon you show so oft your beautiful array

Of silvery bountiful dew drops which sashay

On the shimmering fluid images and hues of blues

Whites, golds, greens and silvery gray!

I wish I could hold you forever

In the blossom of my heart like a firefly

Enjoying your enclosed fiery presence

through the births and deaths of night and day!

I get a knock, a subtle reminder

A gentle shake some day

All these thoughts are but nothing

Except the vagaries of the mind at play!

The truth is, You continue to be with me

 in every, each and every single way

Possible for a mother while tenderly watching

Yet, Pushing Its fledgeling to fly far away!

But the beauty of it all is, that I was

I am and I always will be in you

Whenever, however, wherever I stay

In my inner vision will I find you whenever I seek and pray!

Be Still

By Beth Terrence

Be still as a tree
whose leaves rustle in the breeze
standing firm in the ground
reaching to heaven above
rooted in both worlds
connected
strong
unshakable

*Beth Terrence is a Shaman, Holistic Practitioner and Writer. She
writes regularly on her blog, The Heart Of Awakening: Searching For A
New Paradigm, which offers online transformational resources. Her
story, "Lost & Found: The Birth Of A Shaman", is part of the
collaborative book Inspired Voices: True Stories Of Visionary Women.
Writing poetry is a practice that feeds her soul. Learn more about
Beth at www.bethterrence.com.*

The Fluid Child

By Rani Lee Johnson

"There was a girl, there was a boy.

This was one child.

One night, the child prayed.

Said the child to the Gods:

"Why am I different? I've always wondered why."

 Said the Goddess to the child:

"You are different, you are like the angels in the sky".

 Said the God to the child:

" You are male and female. You are unique, like a star, that is why."

Then the Goddess said:

" You are beautiful, you are gorgeous, you are amazing, you are wonderful."

 Then they said together:

"People are different. People can be evil, they can be cruel. They are just fools!"

 Then the child asked:

"Am I wanted, am I loved? Am I a gift from above?"

 The Gods replied:

" Yes. You are different, you are unique. We can't wait to see you at your peak."

I was born in Little Rock, Arkansas. I grew up in Oak Park, Illinois and currently reside in Missouri. I love to read anything fictional, I am a big fan of Greek/Roman and Norse Mythologies. I have a small artistic side, I love to draw and I love to write about anything that inspires me. I am 28 years old and someday I wish to have my own published and recognized works.

The Dance of the Butterflies
By Janet R. Sady

Happenstance brought me to the meadow.
Monarchs and Swallowtails hovered over sunflowers,
chicory, and purple thistle.
Like delighted children opening birthday packages,
they zipped from blossom to blossom,
dancing as only butterflies know how.
Transfixed—I lingered—cherishing
the magic of this moment.
Dancing butterflies in the midst of an ordinary summer day,
wild and free bringing unexpected pleasure—
gladdening my heart in a special way—
when butterflies danced for me.

On Bended Knee

By Steve Nestor

He was not probing the shadows

Nor planning my demise

He saw something in my ignorance

And nothing in my lies

His patience was a virtue

That I did not deserve

I found joy in the wanderings

Of a unending nerve

Time was ere' escaping

Lost in my misery

Ah too many questions

What did it all mean?

But yea, I finally found him

Or did he find me?

When I stepped outside myself

Alas, on bended knee

Dr. Steve Nestor serves as Senior Pastor for the St. Albans Church of the Nazarene, in St. Albans, WV. He is an accomplished song writer and author; with seven songs professionally recorded. He believes his gift for words is God given, and does not take it lightly. He is married to his partner in ministry Bonnie. They are both cancer survivors, and love the Lord and His church.

Bless the Children

By Pat Yacobucci

Children are precious to you and me

But some parents refuse to see

The spirits of these lively ones are fresh and free and full of laughter

Sometimes so noisy they rattle the rafters.

When they look into your eyes so innocently

Your heart just melts continuously

They count on you for guidance every day

For we are their heroes to show the way.

Treat them well for they are the future

Guide them well, be there for them night and day

Help them grow and send them on their way.

Bless the children and hope for the future is bright

Then sit back and count your blessings each and every night.

God bless the children and their parents.

Are There Answers to Cancer?

By Angela Greenwood

Some people believe they already have the answers that are causing an epidemic called cancer.

Could it be what we are eating or our words that are defeating and not worth repeating?

Could it be an excessive amount of pollution in the air or the negative thoughts we dare to share?

Could it be the results of our actions and fate for all the outer violence and inner hate?

I believe all and more could be put to blame, but there is no need to feel ashamed. Cancer could have been put in our chart...an experience we chose to claim.

Dealing with this disease can cause a great amount of pain. But unless you have already experienced this challenge, it would be difficult to explain.

Cancer can also be a profound wakeup call for us to acknowledge and teach. A renewed spiritual love of life that we might not have otherwise reached.

Even if we do not survive cancer know that we will be healed. Ascending to our real Divine Home, a beauty that will soon be revealed.

So On and On

By Steffan Gilbert

Been burnt at the stake and buried alive;

Been born a prince of compromise;

Seen oh so much yet still alive

It's a grand adventure we're on

Known too much and not lived to tell

Sown seeds of discontent all too well

Grown from each birth to each death knell

It's a grand adventure we're on

And who can say out of the futures of yesterday

Where the Mobius leads on

And why not go with the spiritual labor of play

To where the adventure leads on

Sung my share of resonant songs

Done what was needed to redirect my wrongs

Dowsed the elements with reality's tongs

It's a grand adventure we're on

Steffan Gilbert's work appeared in the recently released anthology, 'I Wonder Why, and his collection of short fiction, 'Stories from the Hollow', is currently available through amazon.com and barnesandnoble.com. He was born in Washington D.C. His career has included stints as a vocational therapist, reporter, and call-in tarot reader. He currently endeavors to persevere as an Ornamental Hermit. A dulcimerist and award winning writer and producer, his material has been performed in comedy clubs and venues across the country, at The National Theater in Washington D.C. and on PBS. He and his wife live in Middle Tennessee.

A Message From Above

By Bernadette Price

For over 50 years

You carried THAT secret deep in your heart

You know you need to heal the past

But when and how do you start?

For the pain of those memories, it seems to last and last

Even though you grew up and had a family that you hold so dear

There are still times that you shed more than a tear

For that little girl who once knew no fear

For Grandad was the adult, and you a mere child

It was at a time when children were seen and not heard

They were to remain meek and mild

"They'll never believe you, go on, "he replied

"say your worst about me, I'll tell them you lied"

So you fought the frustration, the hurt and the pain

You played with your friends, listened to music,

Anything to keep you sane

It worked for some years, this growing up part

But you now cannot ignore this ache in your heart

So you start NOW to heal, it's within your grasp

Your Angels are with you, just trust and see

Let everything go, only then will you be FREE

So go on, dear girl, live your years out

You WERE a good daughter

Of that, there's no doubt

Cotillion

By Jennifer Bateman

A dusting of sadness wrapped up in tranquility;

murmuring madness, awakened divinity.

Vague recollections of wandering peace

with ephemeral seclusion, dictated by chance.

Continuous mercy enveloped in constancy,

whispering choices regained through diplomacy.

Grace reaches out with a gift of release –

an ecstatic dimension, a hope for romance.

What form does your heart take –

what shape will your soul make

when pushed to the limits of love on display?

We won't be mistaken

once fires awaken

and walls of resentment start falling away.

Virtual solitude draping sincerity,

reticent multitudes looking for charity –

searching for favor, and finding a piece

of salvation extended; an offer to dance.

Shedding the Human

By Frederic Wiedemann

On the rooftop patio this particular dawn –

Its oranges and reds ripening without a story –

In the instant, I receive a dangerous vision:

I dream to shed all that is human from me.

To be hostage no longer to thinking,

Nor judging in the compulsive way;

To not even perceive the same as the same old

Within the confines of my constructions.

Oh, to arise as the Beloved:

A fruit nimbly seasoning in the Sun;

Maybe a minnow in the estuary

Pecked into the gizzard of a gull.

To spread through skies as an azure gauze of nimbus clouds;

Or maybe I could change my hardened opinions

Into the purity of a jungle hibiscus;

Or lift as feathers on the thermal warmths.

Since I could not shake off the human

Before I am called to chores,

I gasp for a last gulp of this magic,

As if about to be sucked under the waves

Not knowing how long I might be pinned,

Holding on for as long as I could

This breath

Of freshest Love.

By Frederic Wiedemann, PhD, poet, coach, speaker, world traveler,

and author of Between Two Worlds : The Riddle of Wholeness

and the forthcoming Flash: Sudden & Simple Ways To Feel Connected.

I Am Glad That I Met You

By Andrea Theiszova

My life was filled,
and happy days were upon me,
until you left.

I cried and swear and drunk,
but nothing seemed to help.
I slept and carried on,
and pictured new tomorrows.

But nothing seemed to help.

I exercise and meditate,
and bury myself in work.
Seek crowds and fun,
begging to forget...

But nothing seems to work.

Then only now I realise
I am fucking angry, full of rage.
Embarrassingly hiding face,
the world can`t take me and rejects.

But nothing seems to change.

It slowly kills my intestines,
grotesquely digests all there`s been,
leaving a shell filled with pain,
leaving me lonesome, angry.

But no one seems to note.

Randomly yelling at innocent faces,
relieves my bleeding soul.
The more I give, the more I get,
something to fill in the hole.

Don`t ask me if I am proud on myself,
I wish I could or knew else,
but God had gave me unique freedom,
the way to which is rare.

And no one seems to care.

So take it as my gratitude,
I am glad that I met you,
I might get insane but who cares,
I am happy that we met.

The last Days
By Alberta Felder

The, bible speaks of the last days.
We all need to change our evil ways.
May crimes are committed is your name on heaven's roll, from its gates to be omitted?
Our people are crying, we sit and watch as our young children are dying.
They never participated in a gang but now their lives are taken, in this killing game.
Claiming items that are that are not theirs, robbery is committed before our very eyes, to all to see.
We just sit and watch, how could this be ?
Selling drugs is your hobby.
You sit there, with danger on your mind, in a chair in the lobby.
Another mistaken identity has caused a mother to bury her son, who was just an innocent bystander killed by a gun.
The suspect will be locked up in jail, without bond.
He should get life for the thing he has done.
The mother of the victim is left mourning for her child, only memories left of his precious smile.
Many lives have been corrupted.
No age limit required; killing is the subject.
No matter who is killed, the gang goes untouched, their crimes uninterrupted.
The bullets that enters the bodies fulfill the shooter's desire.
Our neighborhoods are like a war- zone.
The love and respect we once had for one another seems to be gone.
As the world slowly comes to an end, I cannot help but wonder, will I be left a single friend?
Let the people all say amen!

Soma

By Jennifer Bateman

It's the shell that cuts the pattern;

broken shards of shattered hope,

jagged lines entrenched in flesh and bone;

a maze of tangled lies.

It's the brutal blow of vicitmhood

that stings the sky awake;

aching balance brought to clouds of doubt,

obscuring Ancient eyes.

It's the dirty fabric pieced within;

an oily patchwork drenched in sin,

draping me in damning judgment

(surely very wise);

Yet redemption pulses through my soul

while blood flows through my veins.

Even paradise exists

Inside this wreckage that remains.

Hello, it's Me!

By Bernadette Price

They said it wasn't true

They said, "Don't be so daft!

There's no such thing as 'ghosts'

And that, sweetheart, is that!"

Growing up during The Troubles in N.Ireland

Was so difficult, you see

When all I felt was different

I used to wonder, "Why me?"

People to me were colours

Like "the Pink Lady in the hat"

My family would just kindly laugh

And say, "You're as daft as a bat"

But I now know that I saw auras

In all their colourful glory

And I've developed enough to work with Spirit

Now, that doesn't seem too gory!

The road at times has been a challenge

And I have felt like giving up

But my Spirit guides and Angels would tell me,

"Pick yourself up, my Buttercup"

No-one said it was going to be easy

No-one said life's all fun and games

But if you try walking the road less travelled

You will eventually reach your aims

For we are all so unique

God broke the mould after we were born

Our lives are all so different

Some get tattered, some get torn

Never give up, dear child

Be you, be strong, treat yourself kind

For as they say

"Those who mind, don't matter

Those who matter, don't mind"

The Daydream Room

By Megan Moffitt

Waterfalls blurring the vision in my head.

Faceted white sunlight beading on the bed.

"Go away" sign written in red on the door.

Blue jeans and sneakers abandoned on the floor.

Television set blaring in the background.

Drinking so much coffee, I could nearly drowned.

And nothing seems like it wants to go my way.

I don't know how to dance or just what to say.

Picking at loose threads on my shirt to pass time.

I'm feeling like I might be losing my mind.

And that's okay because nobody cares anyway.

Just walking along in the soft summer air,

Miles of clear blue sky falling on my hair.

Singing some song with a dream deep in my heart.

Keeping my head up when it all falls apart.

Biting back a scream when I hate everything.

Stop by the road, listen to the church bells ring.

And no one seems like they want to look away.

I don't know how to act or just what to say.

Wiping the ice cream off the front of my shirt.

Laughing so hard that I cry until it hurts.

And that's okay because nobody minds anyway.

When the moonlight calls and nighttime's beauty breathes,

Run through the streets and go to sleep in the leaves.

Take a moment to feel the earth as it spins.

Dance in to the ocean, wash away your sins.

Lie down in the open arms of a stranger.

Now just close your eyes and forget the danger.

And nothing seems like it wants to stay this way.

I don't know how to speak or what chords to play.

Crying in the dark to the cold stars that shine,

Wishing on every last one that he was mine.

And that's okay because I'll find a way someday.

The Blessing in Death

By Aasiyah I. Farish

We begin dying the moment we are born.

We are dying every moment that we live.

From our very first breath of air,

God begins the countdown.

For every breath with His Name on it, His angels write it down as a good deed.

Every moment that we spend doing good deeds is worth ten times the deed itself!

The traditions tell us that on The Day of Reckoning,

A man will be brought to God who has 99 large scrolls full of the evil things he used to do.

He will be a believing man.

On that Day, he will say that Paradise is not for him,

But Ar-Rehman is most merciful and the man will be forgiven because he believed in The One God.

Faith, the weight of a mustard seed can move mountains,

It can save a man from an eternity of torment.

Subhana'Allah! We are dying every day.

My spirit yearns to be with the prophets and messengers, to learn from them, to pray with them, to prostrate myself to Al-Mu'izz with them!

Die in remembrance of The Only God, Most High and Exalted is He.

This Dunya will be destroyed in the end, like all civilizations
preceding us.

Alhamdulillah, we are dying every day.

*Aasiyah (Sanjivani) Pathak-Farish is a first generation American
Muslim revert who strives to remind youth and elders that God's Love
transcends His Anger, His Mercy is greater than His Wrath, and His
Forgiveness is more abundant than His Vengeance. She was born and
raise in northern California, and loves the beauty of the world that God
hath created. She is currently a full-time student, and is hoping to
enter California State University, Chico's Biological Sciences program
in 2014. She enjoys learning about her faith, and appreciates God and
His Knowledge more through science. Her philosophy is: Knowledge is
Power. In her mind, God is Knowledge and He Alone is Power. Every
day that she breathes, she is thankful for her faith, for her family, and
for the opportunities that she has been given. She remembers, every
day, that when God closes one door, He opens another-- we just have to
find the Light!*

Stay Close To the Valley

By Pol Macmathuna

Stay close to the valley

Wherein your life flows

And you will know only love

And you will know only love

You may go seeking

Or you may be still

You may sit beneath stars

Or climb the highest hill

But stay close to the valley

Wherein your life flows

And you will know only love

And you will know only love

You may find truths

That make you feel whole

You may find lies

That take their toll

But stay close to the valley

Wherein your life flows

And you will know only love

And you will know only love

It is you alone

That can find a way

That leads to fruits

That dont decay

So stay close to the valley

Wherein your life flows

And you will know only love

And you will know only love

For you are a way

And you are your truth

And your gift of life

Is your only proof

So stay close to the valley

Wherein your life flows

And you will know only love

And you will know only love

In Closing...

We hope you have enjoyed the anthology of poetry within this collection. If you were touched by a certain poem, or perhaps by the book as a whole, please do these authors a service and pay it forward by spreading the word with your friends, family, and within your community.

Further, if you enjoyed the collection, we ask you to please consider taking a moment to write a positive review on Amazon.com. This book was written with love in hopes to raise the world's vibration one person at a time. Your time and effort to leave a review will help spread these messages to those who are waiting to be touched by the works of these talented poets.

For more daily inspiration, please visit us at www.spiritualwritersnetwork.com and browse through the many categories that our writers place their submissions into. There is something for everyone at Spiritual Writers Network. If you are an author, aspiring writer, or just someone with a message to share ... please join us! It is free to register, write, and share on our network. Stay tuned for upcoming writing contests as well.

Perhaps *YOU* will be the next author chosen for publication!

TRANSCENDENT PUBLISHING

Do You Have a Book Inside You?

This book was designed, formatted, and published by Transcendent Publishing.

Transcendent Publishing is a one-stop-shop for all your publishing needs. We offer cover design, interior formatting, search engine optimized (SEO) book descriptions, price point consultation, as well as marketing strategies to get your books and in front of your target audience.

In addition to our affordable print-on-demand publishing packages, we also *specialize* in Kindle formatting to ensure your eBook is satisfactory to KDP specifications.

We would love to assist you with your future publishing needs.

Please contact us:

Transcendent Publishing
121 104th Ave Treasure Island, FL 33706
www.transcendentpublishing.com

Transcendent Publishing

9878428R00064

Printed in Great Britain
by Amazon.co.uk, Ltd.,
Marston Gate.